This Little Explore The book belongs to:

_____

For
Curious Learners

Published by Grant Publishing

Sales and Enquires: grantpublishingltd@gmail.com

FOLLOW US ON SOCIAL MEDIA

 @grantpublishingltd

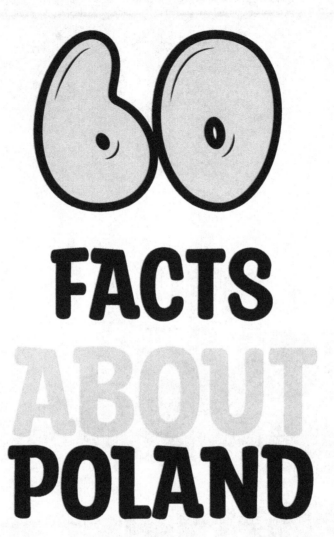

FACTS
ABOUT
POLAND

60 Facts About Poland

Attention, young adventurers! Are you ready to embark on an extraordinary expedition through the enchanting realm of Poland, where history, tradition, and culture intertwine? Get ready to be captivated as we take you on a journey filled with iconic landmarks, charming customs, and delectable culinary delights.

In this captivating book, you will uncover the secrets of Poland's extraordinary heritage.

Let the journey begin!

For Parents

We know that reading a book about a new country can be an exciting adventure for your child. It's important to remember that kids need breaks, and may not want to read the book all in one sitting. Encourage them to take breaks as needed, and ask them questions about what they've learned so far. Discussing the facts with your child can help them remember and retain the information better. You can also use the book as a springboard for further exploration and learning about Poland. Perhaps you can plan a family outing to try some Polish cuisine or visit a local museum with exhibits on Polish culture. Above all, we hope that this book sparks your child's curiosity and inspires them to learn more about the world around them.

MAP

COUNTRY

Poland is a country in the continent of Europe.

Europe is the second-smallest continent in terms of land area but has the third-largest population in the world, with over 740 million people.

Poland is located in central Europe.

Poland is formally known as the Republic of Poland.

The full official name of the Polish state is Rzeczpospolita Polska which translates to "Republic of Poland". The word rzeczpospolita has been used in Poland since at least the 16th century.

The name 'Poland' derives from the Polans, who were a West Slavic tribe who inhabited the Warta River basin of present-day Greater Poland region during the 6th to 8th century.

Dionysus Statue, Poland

Poland is made up of 16 provinces called voivodeships.

Piotrkowska Street, Lodz, Poland

Łódź is a city in central Poland, known as a former textile-manufacturing hub. Its Central Museum of Textiles displays 19th-century machinery, fabrics and handicrafts linked to the trade.

Poland borders Lithuania, Russia, Belarus, Ukraine, Slovakia, the Czech Republic and Germany.

Gdansk, Poland

Bowlowieza Forest, Poland

Poland shares maritime borders with Denmark and Sweden.

Krakow, Poland

Warsaw is the capital city of Poland.

Warsaw is known as the "Phoenix City" due to the number of times it has been destroyed and risen again.

Warsaw is also the largest city.

Warsaw is one of the most congested cities in Europe, with citizens spending an average of 106 hours sitting in traffic every year.

Warsaw is located in the east-central part of Poland.

Marie Curie, who achieved international recognition for her research on radioactivity and was the first female recipient of the Nobel Prize, was born in Warsaw.

Marie Curie

Major cities in Poland include Kraków, Łódź, Wrocław, Poznań, Gdańsk, Szczecin, Bydgoszcz, Lublin and Białystok.

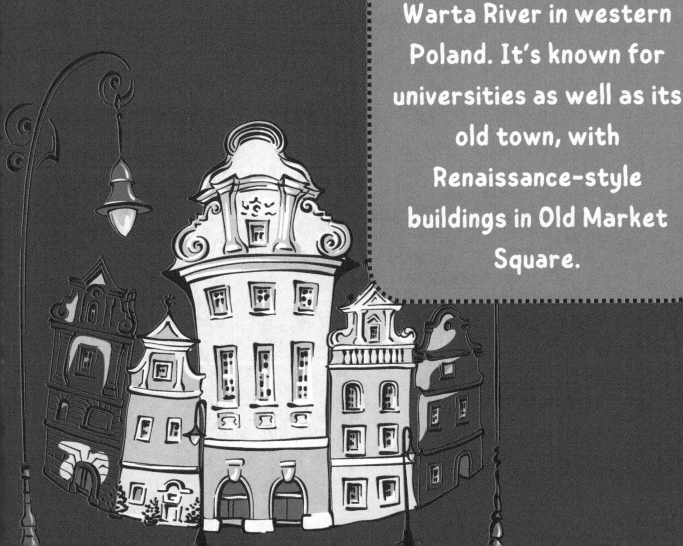

Poznań is a city on the Warta River in western Poland. It's known for universities as well as its old town, with Renaissance-style buildings in Old Market Square.

Poland is 312,696 square kilometres.

Poland is located in the very centre of Europe. With the total area of 312,679 km² (120,728 sq mi) it's the seventh biggest country on the continent.

People from Poland are called Polish or Pole.

The official language of Poland is Polish.

Words in Polish

Good day = Dzień dobry
My name is = Nazywam się
Please = Proszę
Thank you = Dziękuję

Polish is spoken by around 38.7 million people worldwide.

Poland ranks number 37 in the list of countries (and dependencies) by population. The population density in Poland is 134 per Km2 (347 people per mi2).

Poland has a population of around 37 million people.

Poland is the fifth most populous country in the European Union.

Poland has the sixth largest economy in the European Union.

The currency is the Złoty.

The Polish złoty is the official currency and legal tender of Poland. It is subdivided into 100 grosz. It is the most traded currency in Central and Eastern Europe and ranks 21st most-traded in the foreign exchange market.

In Poland, people drive on the right side of the road.

Popular cars in Poland are Skoda, Toyota and Kia.

The national flag of Poland consists of two horizontal stripes of equal width, the upper one white and the lower one red.

The flag is flown continuously on the buildings of the highest national authorities, such as the parliament and the presidential palace.

The national colors, red and white, were officially adopted in 1831.

Poland is a founding member of the United Nations.

The United Nations is an intergovernmental organization whose stated purposes are to maintain international peace and security, develop friendly relations among nations, achieve international cooperation, and serve as a centre for harmonizing the actions of nations.

HISTORY

The first human settlement on Poland dates back to circa 10,000 BC.

In the 10th century, under the Piast dynasty, Poland began to form into a recognisable unitary and territorial entity.

Picture of Piast Castle in Legnica Poland

On 1st September 1939, World War II began with the Nazi German invasion of Poland.

World War II or the Second World War was a global conflict that lasted from 1939 to 1945.

In 2007, Poland joined the Schengen Area which dismantled the countries borders with other EU member states, allowing for full freedom of movement within most of the European Union.

CULTURE

The national anthem of Poland is "Mazurek Dąbrowskiego"

The Polish National Anthem mentions two Polish rivers, the Vistula and the Warta and the French leader, Napoleon Bonaparte. The lyrics also mention a saber as a weapon, giving you an idea about the age of this anthem.

Christianity is the largest religion in Poland.

Picture of Poznan church. Poland

Catholicism is the largest denomination in Poland.

Picture of St Margaret church, Poland

Easter is an important celebration in Poland. On Easter Sunday and Easter Monday all public services such as shops, restaurants, cinemas, galleries and are closed.

Picture of Easter dinner in Poland

Labour Day is a very popular celebration in Poland. Labour Day is celebrated on May 1st and has been a national holiday since the 1950's communist-ruled Poland known as Worker's Day.

Labour Day is a day off for the general population, and schools and most businesses are closed. Many families celebrate the May 1 public holiday with outdoor activities, such as picnics, in Poland.

The crowned white-tailed eagle is a national symbol is often found on clothing, insignia and emblems.

There are 13 government-approved annual public holidays which includes three kings day on 6th January, All Saints' Day on 1 November and independence day on 11th November.

Three Kings Day which is also known as the Epiphany, is a Christian celebration that commemorates the Biblical story of the three kings who followed the star of Bethlehem to bring gifts to the Christ child.

Christmas Eve, though not a public holiday in Poland, is a very special occasion. On the day, people decorate their trees, placed hay under their tablecloth, eat Christmas wafers (opłatek) and have a twelve-dish meatless supper.

People sharing opłatek during a Polish Christmas

Polish music is an integral part of the culture. Popular music genres include folk music, rock, metal, jazz, electronic, and new wave.

Football is the most popular sport in Poland.

Poland has competed in nine FIFA World Cup, with their first appearance being in 1938, where they were eliminated by Brazil.

Volleyball, motorcycle speedway, ski jumping, athletics, American football, handball, basketball, tennis, and combat sport are also popular sports in Poland.

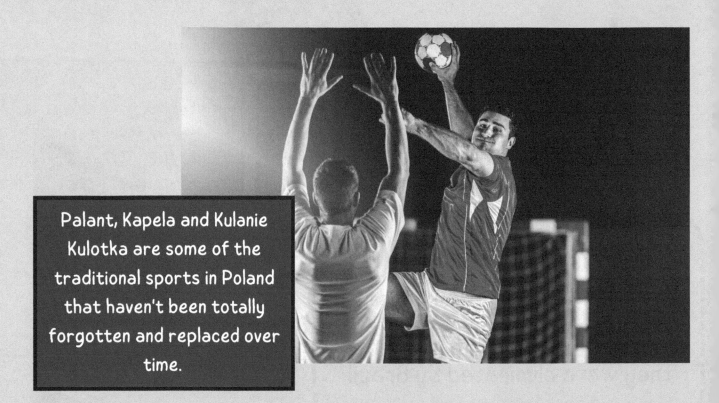

Palant, Kapela and Kulanie Kulotka are some of the traditional sports in Poland that haven't been totally forgotten and replaced over time.

Poland is the birthplace of many renowned composers such as Frédéric Chopin and Artur Rubinstein.

Frédéric François Chopin was a Polish composer and virtuoso pianist of the Romantic period, who wrote primarily for solo piano.

Poland has the youngest age of marriage amongst all the countries in the European Union.

Poland is the birthplace of many notable astronomers such as Nicolaus Copernicus, who established the concept of a heliocentric solar system which posited that the Sun is at the center of the universe.

Nicolaus Copernicus was a Renaissance polymath, active as a mathematician, astronomer, and Catholic canon, who formulated a model of the universe that placed the Sun rather than Earth at its center.

Poland holds the largest open-air music festival in Europe called Pol'and'Rock Festival formerly knows as Woodstock Festival.

CLIMATE

Poland has a temperate climate.

Temperate climates are generally defined as environments with moderate rainfall spread across the year or portion of the year with sporadic drought, mild to warm summers and cool to cold winters

Weather in Poland is characterised by cold winters and warm-hot summers.

The Wawel Cathedral, formally titled the Archcathedral Basilica of Saint Stanislaus and Saint Wenceslaus, is a Catholic cathedral situated on Wawel Hill in Kraków, Poland.

January is the coldest month in Poland.

The warmest month in Poland is July.

Mount Rysy is the highest point of Poland.

Rysy is a mountain in the crest of the High Tatras, eastern part of the Tatra Mountains, lying on the border between Poland and Slovakia.

There are 30 rivers in Poland.

Poland is one of the European countries having many beautiful rivers. Poland has 30 rivers including major rivers, small rivers, tributaries.

Notable rivers of Poland are the Wda, Brda, Drwęca, Bzura, Narew, Wkra, Bug, Biebrza, Pilica and Wieprz.

Picture of The River Wda

Poland has many lakes which includes Lake Sniardwy, which is the countries largest lake.

Picture of Lake Sniardwy

Poland has a wide range of insect, bird and mammal species.

The white-tailed eagle is the national animal of Poland.

The white-tailed eagle, sometimes known as the 'sea eagle', is a very large bird of prey, widely distributed across temperate Eurasia.

Common animals found in Poland include beavers, wolves, lynxes, and brown bears.

CUISINE

Bigos stew is the national dish of Poland. It is a hearty stew made with meat.

Polish cuisine contains a lot of grains and roots, vegetables.

Tłusty Czwartek, or "Fat Thursday", is a Polish culinary custom on the last Thursday before Lent. Traditionally, it is an occasion to enjoy sweets and cakes before the forty days of abstinence expected of Catholics until Easter Day.

A popular dish in Poland is Schabowy which is a pork chop coated in breadcrumbs.

Popular meals in Poland include kiełbasa, pierogi, pyzy, kopytka, gołąbki, śledzie, bigos, schabowy and oscypek.

Kielbasa is any type of meat sausage from Poland and a staple of Polish cuisine.

The drink 'Vodka' originated in Poland.

Glossary

Castle
Poland has many old castles.

Chopin
A famous composer and pianist from Poland whose music is still loved today.

Christmas Eve
Wigilia is a special Polish Christmas Eve dinner with many traditions, like sharing a special wafer called "opłatek."

Easter
Święconka is a Polish Easter tradition where families bring baskets of food to church to be blessed.

Flag
The flag of Poland consists of two horizontal stripes - white on top and red on the bottom.

Gdansk
A port city in Poland known for its maritime history.

Kielbasa
A tasty Polish sausage that comes in many different flavors.

Krakow
Another famous city in Poland known for its historical significance and beautiful architecture.

Language
Polish is the official language of Poland, and the book can introduce a few basic words and phrases.

Pierogi
A delicious Polish dumpling

Author's Note

Dear young readers,

I am so excited to have shared with you all about Poland, a country that is rich in history, art and culture. As an author, I am always inspired by the incredible diversity and beauty of the world around us, and I hope this book has inspired you to explore and learn more about Poland.

I was inspired to write this book because I believe that learning about different cultures and countries can help us understand and appreciate the world better. It's so important to celebrate and learn from different traditions and ways of life, and I hope this book has helped you do just that.

If you enjoyed reading this book, I would love it if you could leave a review on Amazon. Reviews help other readers discover the book and can make a big difference for independent authors like myself.
Thank you for joining me on this journey, and I hope this book has sparked your curiosity and imagination. Keep exploring and learning about the world around you!

Sincerely,
Grant Publishing

Made in United States
Orlando, FL
03 December 2024

54911319R00043